The Old
GET WELL
POSTCARD BOOK

A Sterling/Main Street Book
Sterling Publishing Co., Inc. New York

10 9 8 7 6 5 4 3 2 1

A Sterling/Main Street Book

Copyright © 1992 by Sterling Publishing
Published by Sterling Publishing Company, Inc.
387 Park Avenue South, New York, N.Y. 10016
Distributed in Canada by Sterling Publishing
% Canadian Manda Group, P.O. Box 920, Station U
Toronto, Ontario, Canada M8Z 5P9
Distributed in Great Britain and Europe by Cassell PLC
Villiers House, 41/47 Strand, London WC2N 5JE, England
Distributed in Australia by Capricorn Link Ltd.
P.O. Box 665, Lane Cove, NSW 2066

Manufactured in Hong Kong
All rights reserved

ISBN 0-8069-8766-9

Hoping You May Soon Be Well.

Get Well Soon

Post Card

Whitney Made Worcester Mass

From *The Old-Fashioned Get Well Postcard Book* © by Sterling Publishing Co., Inc.

Post Card

From *The Old-Fashioned Get Well Postcard Book* © by Sterling Publishing Co., Inc.

Get Well Soon

Get Well Greetings

POST CARD

From *The Old-Fashioned Get Well Postcard Book* © by Sterling Publishing Co., Inc.

POST CARD

From *The Old-Fashioned Get Well Postcard Book* © by Sterling Publishing Co., Inc.

Wishing You a Speedy Recovery

Feel Better Soon

Post Card

Whitney Made Worcester Mass

From *The Old-Fashioned Get Well Postcard Book* © by Sterling Publishing Co., Inc.

Post Card

From *The Old-Fashioned Get Well Postcard Book* © by Sterling Publishing Co., Inc.

237

Sincere Get Well Wishes

Get Well Soon

POST CARD

From *The Old-Fashioned Get Well Postcard Book* © by Sterling Publishing Co., Inc.

POST CARD

From *The Old-Fashioned Get Well Postcard Book* © by Sterling Publishing Co., Inc.

Feel Better Soon

Get Well Wishes

Post Card

Whitney Made Worcester Mass

From *The Old-Fashioned Get Well Postcard Book* © by Sterling Publishing Co., Inc.

Post Card

From *The Old-Fashioned Get Well Postcard Book* © by Sterling Publishing Co., Inc.

Sincere Get Well Wishes

Hoping You May Soon Be Well.

189B

POST CARD

From *The Old-Fashioned Get Well Postcard Book* © by Sterling Publishing Co., Inc.

POST CARD

From *The Old-Fashioned Get Well Postcard Book* © by Sterling Publishing Co., Inc.

Get Well Soon

Get Well Wishes

Post Card

Whitney Made Worcester Mass

From *The Old-Fashioned Get Well Postcard Book* © by Sterling Publishing Co., Inc.

Post Card

From *The Old-Fashioned Get Well Postcard Book* © by Sterling Publishing Co., Inc.

Get Well Greetings

Get Well Soon

POST CARD

From *The Old-Fashioned Get Well Postcard Book* © by Sterling Publishing Co., Inc.

POST CARD

From *The Old-Fashioned Get Well Postcard Book* © by Sterling Publishing Co., Inc.

Get Well Greetings

Get Well Wishes

POST CARD

From *The Old-Fashioned Get Well Postcard Book* © by Sterling Publishing Co., Inc.

POST CARD

From *The Old-Fashioned Get Well Postcard Book* © by Sterling Publishing Co., Inc.

Get Well Greetings

Hope You'll Soon Be Up and Around

Post Card

Whitney Made Worcester Mass

From *The Old-Fashioned Get Well Postcard Book* © by Sterling Publishing Co., Inc.

Post Card

From *The Old-Fashioned Get Well Postcard Book* © by Sterling Publishing Co., Inc.

Get Well Wishes

Feel Better Soon

POST CARD

From *The Old-Fashioned Get Well Postcard Book* © by Sterling Publishing Co., Inc.

POST CARD

From *The Old-Fashioned Get Well Postcard Book* © by Sterling Publishing Co., Inc.

Feel Better Soon

Get Well Greetings

Post Card

Whitney Made Worcester Mass

From *The Old-Fashioned Get Well Postcard Book* © by Sterling Publishing Co., Inc.

Post Card

From *The Old-Fashioned Get Well Postcard Book* © by Sterling Publishing Co., Inc.

Sincere Get Well Wishes

Hope You'll Soon Be Up and Around

POST CARD

From *The Old-Fashioned Get Well Postcard Book* © by Sterling Publishing Co., Inc.

POST CARD

From *The Old-Fashioned Get Well Postcard Book* © by Sterling Publishing Co., Inc.

Sincere Get Well Wishes

Feel Better Soon

Post Card

Whitney Made Worcester Mass

From *The Old-Fashioned Get Well Postcard Book* © by Sterling Publishing Co., Inc.

Post Card

From *The Old-Fashioned Get Well Postcard Book* © by Sterling Publishing Co., Inc.

Get Well Wishes

Get Well Soon

POST CARD

From *The Old-Fashioned Get Well Postcard Book* © by Sterling Publishing Co., Inc.

POST CARD

From *The Old-Fashioned Get Well Postcard Book* © by Sterling Publishing Co., Inc.

Get Well Soon

Get Well Soon

POST CARD

From *The Old-Fashioned Get Well Postcard Book* © by Sterling Publishing Co., Inc.

POST CARD

From *The Old-Fashioned Get Well Postcard Book* © by Sterling Publishing Co., Inc.